STOP Meowing AND GO THE F*CK TO SLEEP

by Rosa Silva

Stop meowing and go the f*ck to sleep
Copyright © 2016 by Rosa Silva

Illustrated by Diana Necsulescu

ISBN-13: 978-1540697653
ISBN-10: 1540697657

Printed in USA

For Mr. Cat, who wouldn't let me have a good night's sleep for months

The stars are shining brightly in the velvet sky.
A solitary owl is hooting deep.
Children are tucked in for the night.
So, please stop meowing, and go the f*ck to sleep!

At 10 a.m., you doze off.
At noon, you take a nap.
At 4 p.m., it's siesta time.
At 4 a.m., I want to sleep, and you don't give a crap!

Stop scratching the door.
I will not let you in.
Stop scratching the door, stop scratching the door...
For God's sake, get in!

Stop licking my nose.
Stop licking my hair.
Stop licking my toes.
This is not a love affair!

Here is your favorite catnip toy.
Take some of these yummy treats.
Now, do you know what I would enjoy?
If you would go the f*ck to sleep!

Maybe you think you are in the jungle;
that you are a tiger chasing a wild ox.
Well, I've got news for you.
You are a pet who sleeps in a bed and craps in a box!

You don't need to hunt.
Your food is served to you on a plate.
So, I'll have to be blunt.
You are not a tiger, you are a pussycat who needs to lose some weight!

Take that wand toy away.
It's too late to play.
No, I don't want that mouse.
I just want to be the boss of my own house.

What are you meowing for?
Why are you giving me that look?
You know you are the cat I adore,
but please, stop meowing, and go the f*ck to sleep!

I have to get up early tomorrow.
I must get to work on time,
so I can earn some dough
to buy expensive toys that you will ignore.

Stop making biscuits on my belly.
What are you doing on top of the telly?
For heaven's sake, just close your eyes,
and go the f*ck to sleep!

MEOW!

Finally, you're lying down across my ankles.
Your eyes are beginning to shut.
Now I thank God for his mercy,
as I get myself ready to sleep.

The night is finally silent.
The solitary owl is hooting deep.
I can blissfully rest my head on the pillow,
'cause you finally went the f*ck to sleep!

I'm dreaming of a sunny garden.
A cat is approaching in the distance.
MEOW! It's you again! You have got to be kidding.
Please go the f*ck back to sleep!

Made in the USA
Columbia, SC
05 December 2017